T0190921

ALL THE DAUGHTERS OF THE EARTH

세상의 모든 딸들

All the Daughters of the Earth

Published in 2023 by Seoul Selection U.S.A., Inc.
4199 Campus Drive, Suite 550, Irvine, CA 92612
Phone: 949-509-6584 / Seoul office: 82-2-734-9567
Fax: 949-509-6599 / Seoul office: 82-2-734-9562
Email: hankinseoul@gmail.com
Website: www.seoulselection.com

ISBN: 978-1-62412-152-4
Printed in the Republic of Korea

ALL THE DAUGHTERS OF THE EARTH

세상의 모든 딸들

김일연 시집

KIM ILYEON
Sijo Poems

Translated by Brother Anthony of Taizé

Seoul Selection

꽃은
눈멀어
몸을 다 연다

그마저 없다 하면
봄가을
우예 살꼬

눈머는 그 깊이 아니면
무엇을 하리

짧은 날을

2023년 봄
김일연

Since flowers are

blind

they open their bodies fully.

Without that

how could they live through

spring and autumn?

Without the depth of that blindness

what can they do?

A short day.

Spring 2023

Kim Ilyeon

CONTENTS • 차례

2

3

4

ALL THE DAUGHTERS OF THE EARTH 세상의 모든 딸들 ALL THE DAUGHTERS OF THE EARTH 세상의 모든 딸들

PART
I

딸

짐 빼고 집 내놓고
용돈 통장 해지하고

내 번호만 적혀 있는
휴대전화 정지하고

남기신 경로우대증 품고
울고 나니 적막하다

A Daughter

Taking her things and leaving the house,
after closing the bank account,

terminating her mobile phone
where only my number was saved,

pocketing the senior pass I'd inherited,
feeling lonely after tears.

별

연필을 깎아주시던 아버지가 계셨다

밤늦도록 군복을 다리던 어머니가 계시고

마당엔 흑연빛 어둠을 벼리는 별이 내렸다

총알 스치는 소리가 꼭 저렇다 하셨다

물뱀이 연못에 들어 소스라치는 고요

단정한 필통 속처럼 누운 가족이 있었다

A Star

Father used to sharpen pencils.

Mother used to iron military uniforms late into the night and a star sharpening graphite-black darkness came down into the yard.

I was told that the sound of bullets grazing past was exactly the same.

A silence terrified by a water snake entering a pond and the family was there as if lying in a tidy pencil case.

어머니

비바람 눈보라에 제일 먼저 닿는
탑신

제일 밑바닥에 남아 사람 만드는
초석

온몸이
모서리가 된
둥근 이름
어머니

Mother

Pagoda body

first struck by rain and snow.

Foundation stone

remaining at the lowest point and making people.

Well-rounded name,

its whole body

become a corner:

Mother.

수묵

달밤 함석지붕이 부서지게 환하고
낡은 창호 봉창이 찢어지게 환하면
어머니 싱가 재봉틀 실밥 쌓이던 소리

적막의 솜이불이 동화처럼 덮이고
무지근한 눈두덩이 맷돌처럼 눌리면
돌돌돌 싱가 재봉틀 세상 끝 구르던 소리

Ink

The sound of Mother's Singer sewing machine piling up
stitches
as the tin roof shone shatteringly bright on moonlit nights,
and the old paper covering doors and windows shone
tearingly bright.

The throbbing sound of her Singer sewing machine rolling
on to the end of the world
as the blanket of silence covered me like a fairy tale,
and my heavily-lidded eyes are pressed down like a
millstone.

극락강*

극락강 가에 앉아
어머니와 나와

아기를 들쳐 업고 기저귀 보따리 안고

가난한 어린 엄마가
앉아 울던 그 강가에

옛이야기 나누며
어머니와 나와

한참을 울다 돌아가 다시 살던 타관 땅

강 너머
극락을 가는
구름 가마에 앉아

* 광주에 있는 강 이름

Geungnakgang[*]

Mother and me
sitting together by Geungnakgang River.

That riverside where my poor young mother
sat and cried.

Picked up the baby and held the diaper bag.

Mother and me
sharing old stories together.

That foreign land we returned to live in after crying for a
long time.

Sitting in a cloud palanquin
going to Paradise
over the river.

---

[*] Geungnakgang is a river in the city of Gwangju. *Geungnak* is a
Buddhist term for paradise.

만추

가득하고 묵직하게 달이 찼다 만삭이다
젖 먹던 힘을 다해 네 힘껏 밀어내렴

마지막 혼을 넣듯이 가을볕은 쏟아지고

어머니가 될 일 몸 풀 일만 남은 들판
해산 온 딸에게서 혈육을 받아내듯

해종일 할머니 혼자 가을을 받으시고

Late Autumn

Full and heavy, the pregnancy is at full term.
Push with all your might.

As if making one final effort, the autumn sunlight pours
down.

Fields with only delivery left to become a mother,
as if gaining flesh and blood from the daughter come
home to give birth.

All day long, grandmother alone receiving autumn.

잿등

고구마밭 따라서 탱자 울을 지나면
어둑해진 정지 앞 감나무에 부엉이
떠나온 외할머니 그리워 눈물짓는 어머니

암탉을 물고 가는 파란 늑대 발꿈치
삽짝에 눈 한 덩이 떨어지는 겨울밤
병들어 마른 얼굴로 돌아눕는 아버지

Mountain Ridge

Once past the spiny orange hedge following the sweet potato field,

an owl on a persimmon tree in front of a dim kitchen,

Mother weeping for her departed mother.

Heels of a blue wolf running off carrying a hen,

one winter's night when a load of snow is falling on the gateway,

as father, sick, turns over with a gaunt face.

잠옷

고단히 내 돌아와 웅크려 잠이 들매

융 몇 마 끊으시어 눈어림을 하신다

바늘귀 더듬으시는 맘이 자꾸 급하여

앞가림 못하는 걸 알아보신 어머니

그리움 깊을수록 인생살이 쓸쓸하다고

아직도 네가 춥구나 잠옷을 만드신다

Pajamas

I come back, weary, curl up and fall asleep.

She cuts off a few feet of flannel and makes a rough estimate.

Ever impatient, her heart keeps fumbling at the needle's eye.

Mother knows I am not taking good care of myself.

The deeper the yearning, the lonelier the life, she says.

Still you're cold! So she makes pajamas.

관음 어머니

동대문 시장 가서 옷 사 입혀드리고
멀찍이 떨어져서 뒤돌아보시라 하며
참 좋다
참 좋다 하시는
어머니를 보는 일

아래로
흐르고 계신 어머니 관음님의
눈가에 비어지는 눈물도 눈물이거니
비싼 옷 저어하시는 마음에도
젖는 것을

선재동자가 관음을 뵈옵는 것도 그렇지만
내가 어머니 되고 어머니 할머니 되어
환하게 마주 서 웃는
이날이
좋지 않으랴

Mother Guanyin

Seeing Mother
after we went to Dongdaemun Market and bought clothes
for her to wear, telling her to look back from a few steps
behind,
saying: Great,
really great.

The tears
emerging from the corners of Mother Guanyin's eyes as
she flows on down
are really tears
soaking a heart
afraid for expensive clothes.

Little Sudhana seeing Guanyin is the same, but
isn't this day
when I become Mother, and Mother becomes grandmother
all standing smiling brightly at each other
really great?

내 생애 토란

철 지난 남방셔츠 초보 농군 아버지
시내버스 시외버스 시내버스 갈아타고
키우신 토란 한 자루 종일 지고 오셨지

잠긴 문밖에서 늦도록 기다리셨지
토란국 보글보글 끓여드리기라도 하지
알토란 한번 맛있게 조려 먹기라도 하지

베란다 한구석에 그대로 썩히고 만
그 자루 끌어안고 한바탕 울어봤으면
아버지 가시고 나서 슬픈 내 생애 토란

My Life's Taro

Novice farmer Father with his unseasonal sports shirt
took an inner-city bus then an intercity bus, then an inner-
city bus,
spent a whole day bringing a sack of taro that he had
grown.

Maybe he waited until late outside the locked door.
I should have boiled taro soup for him,
I should have cooked taro for myself to eat deliciously.

If only I had taken out and hugged that sack
as it lay rotting in a corner of the veranda
after Father passed away, my sad life's taro.

국숫집에서

어머니와 마주 앉아 국수를 먹었습니다

해 좋은 유리창 밖 밀물처럼 오는 봄

새들이 날아가는 소리 호르륵호륵 내면서

한 그릇 다 드시고 매콤해서 별미로구나

철쭉꽃에 겹치는 주름꽃 환한 웃음이

쭈르륵 미끄러지는 인라인스케이트 타고서

At the Noodle Restaurant

I sat facing Mother and ate noodles.

Spring was coming in like the tide outside the sunny window,

birds were making flapping sounds as they went flying.

Eat a whole bowl, it's spicy, it's a specialty.

Her bright smile, wrinkles overlapping with azaleas,

went sliding by on gliding inline skates.

성인(聖人)

못생기고
재미없고
배경 없고
능력 없는

나 만나 다 늙었다고 아내 등 쓸어줍니다

나 만나 고생했다고 남편 손 잡아줍니다

A Saint

Ugly,

no fun,

no background,

incompetent as I am,

I rub my wife's back, saying "You've grown old since you

first met me."

She takes her husband's hand, saying, "You've had a hard

time since you first met me."

꽁치 한 마리

아홉 마리 삼천 원에 떨이로 산 꽁치를

소금 뿌려 차곡차곡 갈무리해 얼려놓고

작은 놈 한 마리 구워 저녁상을 보신다

어둠 내려앉으면 원양(遠洋) 같은 열네 평

같이 먹잘 이도 없이 한 벌 수저 소리만

어머니, 적막강산이 바다를 잡수신다

One Saury

Nine saury bought at a marked-down price for 3,000 won.

Sprinkled with salt, arranged in a neat pile and frozen,

a small one, fried, adorns the dinner table.

When darkness falls, the modest space is like the open
sea.

With no one to eat with, only the sound of cutlery,

Mother sadly eats the sea.

헛꽃

나의 괴로움 한갓 투정에 불과하고

나의 절망은
한갓
거짓에 불과한 것을

어머니 가시고 나서야
나는
깨달았어요

Fruitless Flower

My suffering is nothing but whining,

my despair
is nothing
but lies.

It was only after Mother died
that I
realized that.

향수

남녘 바닷가에서 주워 온 작은 몽돌
책상 서랍 구석에 버려져 있는 너를
네 고향 모래밭으로 데려다주고 싶다

손잡고 거닐었던 어머닌 가셨지만
품속에 안겨보는 아이의 그 기쁨을
나처럼 늦지 않았다면 돌려주고 싶다

Nostalgia

You small pebbles found on the southern coast
and left behind in a corner of a desk drawer,
I want to take you back to the sands of your home.

The mother I used to walk hand in hand with is gone
but if it's not too late, like me, I want to give back
the happiness of the child snuggled in her arms.

뉴욕에 있는 딸에게

너와 아가 모두 무탈하길 소원하며

아마존의 유모차를 마천루의 정글로

열 달을 고르고 골라 실한 것으로 보낸다

To My Daughter in New York

Hoping that you and the baby are okay,

I'm sending a stroller from Amazon to the skyscraper jungle city,

a stroller that I spent ten months choosing, a sturdy one.

저녁이 깊어지면
– J의 그림에 부침

산그늘 서늘하고 바람 거칠어지는
두고 온 골짜기에 하얗게 억새가 피면
억새가 거기 있음을 추억하는 이 있겠지

식은 차를 데우고 나는 여기 책을 읽고
당신은 비스듬히 거기 음악을 듣고
가끔은 저무는 밖을 내다보기도 하겠지

발이 부르트도록 먼 길을 걸어와서
고요하게 흐르는 강물이 된 그 사람
고통도 기쁨이었음을 기억하는 이 있겠지

When the Evening Deepens

—Regarding J's Picture

In the valley I left behind the mountain shade is cool, the
wind is rough
and as the pampas grass blooms white
there is surely one who remembers that there is pampas
grass there.

As I warm cold tea and sit here reading a book,
while you listen to music over there,
sometimes we will look out at the setting sun.

Having walked a long way until his feet were swollen,
he became a quietly flowing river.
There is surely one who remembers that even pain was
joy.

오동도 동백꽃

어제는 하늘 끝까지 갔다가 되돌아오고

오늘은 바다 끝까지 갔다가 되돌아와요

붉은 꽃 더 붉게 지면 당신을 잊을까요

Odongdo's* Camellias

Yesterday I went to the end of the sky and came back.

Today I go to the end of the sea and come back.

When the red flowers become redder and fall, will I forget you?

* Odongdo is a small island in the harbor of Yeosu, Jeollanam-do, famed for its camellias.

ALL THE DAUGHTERS OF THE EARTH 세상의 모든 딸들 ㅍ ALL THE DAUGHTERS OF THE EARTH 세상의 모든 딸들 ALL THE DAUGHTERS OF THE EARTH 세상의 모든 딸들 ALL THE DAUGHTERS OF THE EARTH 세상의 모든 딸들 ㅍ ALL THE DAUGHTERS OF THE EARTH 세상의 모든 딸들 ALL THE DAUGHTERS OF THE EARTH 세상의 모든 딸들 ALL THE DAUGHTERS OF THE EARTH 세상의 모든 딸들 ALL THE DAUGHTERS OF THE EARTH 세상의 모든 딸들 ALL THE DAUGHTERS OF THE EARTH 세상의 모든 딸들 ALL THE DAUGHTERS OF THE EARTH 세상의 모든 딸들 ALL THE DAUGHTERS OF THE EARTH 세상의 모든 딸들

PART
2

해

캄캄한 동굴에서
춤을 시작한 집시

어둠 속의 춤이라야
진품의 춤이 된다

사방이 어둠이어도
해는
네 안에 있다

The Sun

A gypsy began to dance
in a dark cave.

Only a dance in the dark
can become
a genuine dance.

Even if it's dark everywhere,
the sun
is within you.

생명

미끄러져 들어온 눈부신 섬광 한 점

물까치 어린 날개는 연한 하늘색이다

깃털에 흐르는 빛이 공단보다 보드랍다

공단보다 보드라운 그 빛, 봉황처럼

이제 막 시작하는 재롱을 감싸고 있다

홰치는 느릅나무에 잎사귀가 솟을 때

Life

A dazzling flash of light that slipped in.

The magpie's young wings are a light sky-blue.

The light flowing through the feathers is softer than satin.

That light softer than satin is wrapping, like a phoenix,

the cute tricks that are about to begin,

when the leaves sprout on each fluttering elm tree.

첫사랑

박태기나무에서는 풋사과 향이 나요

풋사과 향 목소리로 작은 새가 울어요

나무의 가슴팍에서 날아가지 않아요

First Love

The hawthorn tree gives off a smell of green apples.

A little bird cries with a green apple-scented voice.

It refuses to fly away from the heart of the tree.

만개

네 눈길이 닿으면 소스라치는 허공

그때에 못했던 말 지금도 말할 수 없어

참았던 울음보 터져
쏟아내는
꽃송이들

Full Bloom

When your eyes touch it, the appalling void.

Unable to say the words that couldn't be said then.

The fit of tears that had been held back bursts forth.
Flowers
pouring out.

절리

끊임없는 파도가 너를 만들었다
내리꽂는 칼날보다 거센 비바람이
상처를 가슴에 안고 꼿꼿이 서게 했다

A Rock Pillar

The endless waves made you.

Rain and wind stronger than slashing blades

made you stand upright, holding those wounds to your

breast.

봄꿈

나무의 높이만큼 목이 길어지는

과부하의 심장이 아픈 줄도 모르고

우듬지 새로 핀 잎을 먹고 싶은 기린

Spring Dream

Its neck stretches out as long as the height of a tree,

unaware that its overloaded heart is aching,

a giraffe eager to eat leaves freshly sprouting on a treetop.

하늘과 호수

하늘은 제 얼굴을 가을 호수에 씻고
호수는 제 얼굴을 가을 하늘에 닦고
서로가 맑고 넓고 깊은 거울을 들여다본다

Sky and Lake

The sky washes its face in the autumn lake,

the lake wipes its face on the autumn sky,

then each looks into the other's clear, wide, deep mirror.

갈림길

오르락내리락하는 능선에 땀 흘릴까

물 보고 꽃 보면서 쉽고 편하게 갈까

한 길로 길을 잡으면 다른 길 버려야 한다

A Crossroads

Shall I sweat on undulating ridges?

Shall I walk easily and comfortably looking at water and flowers?

If I take one path, I have to give up the other path.

풍장

윤기 도는 지렁이가 풀밭에 나와 있다

한참 지나 다시 봐도 가만히 누워 있다

햇볕에 몸은 마르는데 산새 깍깍 우는데

땅 위에
하늘 아래
장마 끝 환한 풀잎에

비이슬 묻어 있는 바람결 귀를 묻고

제 몸을 비우고 있는 크고 검은 지렁이

Wind Burial

A shiny earthworm is out on the grass.

After a while, I look back. It's lying still.

Its body is drying in the sun, while the birds are croaking.

On the ground
under the sky
on a bright blade of grass at the end of the rainy season.

Its ears buried in the wind, full of rain and dew,

A big black earthworm emptying itself.

고니의 잠

뽀족한 부리는 날개 밑에 접어두고

둥글게 구부린 목은 몸속으로 묻었다

한없이 내면을 향한 원형(原形)의 시간이 있다

A Swan Asleep

The pointed beak folded under a wing,

its curved neck buried in its body,

original time infinitely turned inward.

폭포

산이 높을수록 까마득한 물의 깊이

가는 길 험하다고 주저할 일 있을까

절경은 뛰어들면서 만드는 것이라오

A Waterfall

The higher the mountain, the deeper the distant water.

Are you hesitant because the path ahead is rough?

Superb views are created by jumping in.

시월

철새들이 딛고 가는 깊고 푸른 물동이

차란차란 넘치게 물너울 출렁였으나

새들이 떠나고 나면 잠잠히 돌아오곤 했다

발자국 하나 남김없이 지우는 계절이었다

저 깊은 가없음을 관(冠)처럼 머리에 이고

모과는 고독해야만 향기를 머금는 것이다

October

A deep, blue water jar briefly frequented by migrating birds,

brimming full, overflowing, wavelets rocking, but

once the birds have left, quietly growing still.

It was the season for every last footprint to be erased.

Wearing that deep expanse on its head like a crown,

the quince only retains its fragrance in solitude.

미나리아재비와 애기똥풀*

너는
나인 듯이
나는 너인 듯이 서서

해 났다 햇빛 쬐자 눈물 담고 웃는다

여기서 돌아가지 말자

산언덕에
나란히

* 두 풀꽃은 외양이 매우 닮아 종종 혼동되기도 한다.

Buttercup and Celandine*

You
stand as if you were me
and I as if I were you.

The sun's shining. Let's bask in the sunlight. We laugh,
holding back tears.

Let's not leave here.

On the hill,
side by side.

* The two flowers are very similar in appearance and are often
confused.

꽃 화분

솜사탕만 한 꽃 화분을 놓았다

틈새 없이 부풀은 꽃잎들이 바다였다

그 꽃을 보는 날마다 내 마음이 바다였다

A Flower Pot

I prepared a flower pot the size of a ball of cotton candy.

The petals that expanded without leaving a gap were the sea.

Every day I saw that flower, my heart was the sea.

새벽달

만 리 밖에 바람 보내고
서러운 건 보내고

내 뜨락
빈 가지에
금지환을 끼우며

녹슨 문
열어달라고
들어가고 싶다고

Dawn Moon

Sending the wind to blow a ten thousand ri away
sending away everything sad.

Slipping a gold ring
onto an empty branch
in my garden.

It begs me to open
the rusty door
as it wants to come in.

입추

밤 더위에 길고양이 아옹아옹 하더니

첫새벽 소나기 긋고 비둘기 구구 난다

싱싱한 매미 울겠다 들 잎사귀 산 잎사귀

이 비 다 그치고 산막 깨끗해지고

짙어진 밤이슬에 코스모스 젖는 날

앞 냇물 가을 잔고기들 환한 속 보이겠다

Autumn Begins

In the heat of night, stray cats wail.

At first light, showers fall and pigeons coo,

fresh cicadas will cry. Leaves in fields, leaves in hills,

once this rain stops the mountain hut will be clean,

days when the cosmos flowers are soaked with heavy
night-time dew

and in a nearby stream small fish of autumn can be
glimpsed in brightness.

와불

개미도 건너가고 바람도 쉬어 가는

새똥이 묻어 있는 펑퍼짐한 돌덩이

자비도 관능도 버리고 드디어 해방되었소

Reclining Buddha

The ants cross it, the wind rests on it,

a flat rock with bird droppings on it,

abandoning mercy and desires, it finally achieves emancipation.

ALL THE DAUGHTERS OF THE EARTH 세상의 모든 딸들 ALL THE DAUGHTERS OF THE EARTH 세상의 모든 딸들

PART
3

아리랑 변주

불붙은 솔가리가 별사탕빛을 내면
장작을 고아놓고 큰 숨 들이쉬고
붕붕붕 눈 질끈 감고 풍구를 돌렸다

무너진 울안으로 성큼 들어온 어둠
모과나무 잡아먹고 정지 문에 서성일 때
두 팔이 빠져라 하고 풍구를 돌렸다

장작불이 피었다 도깨비야 나가라
휘휘한 뒤꼍에서 부엉이가 울 때쯤엔
난쟁이 소리가락도 가물가물 이었다

해 지고 허리 펴는 어둑한 밭두렁을
삼실같이 이어진 구성진 골목길을
엄니는 돌아오겠네 아라리 아라리요

Arirang Variations

When the flaming pine needles were glowing like star
candy
I added firewood and took a big breath,
closed my eyes tightly and worked the bellows.

When the darkness that came striding over the fallen
fence
had consumed the quince tree and was lingering at the
kitchen door
I used both arms and worked the bellows.

The bonfire blossomed, goblins away!
By the time the owl cried from the desolate hill behind
The faint singing of the dwarf began.

Along the dim field banks where she can stretch her back
after sunset,
along the harmonious alleyways like threads of hemp,
Mother is coming back. *Arari arariyo.*❶

❶ *Arari arariyo*: the refrain of the Korean national song "Arirang"

*

풍진세상 어디에 파랑새가 있더냐
돌아야 사는 바람개비 삶이었다

어울려 어우른 무늬
빚어내는 강강술래

*

서러운 신명이야 내림인 것이지

날라리 장구 꽹과리 쏟아붓는 소내기

미어져 터지는 마당
비워내는 징 소리

*

Where in these worldly cares were there ever bluebirds?

Ours was a pinwheel life that had to turn.

Harmonized,

linked, a pattern

produced by *ganggangsullae*.❷

*

A sad excitement is a kind of possession.

A downpour of *nallari* sounds, *janggu, kkwaenggwari*,❸

overwhelming, bursting out, celebration,

draining gong sound.

❷ *Ganggangsullae*: a traditional Korean round dance

❸ *Nallari, janggu, kkwaegwari*: traditional Korean instruments

사랑도 내 사랑은 자진모리 숨 가쁜데
속 타는 님 사랑은 진양조로 넘는다
보시게 굽이굽이에 추임새나 넣어주

내려치며 꺾이며 잉아 걸어 내닫는다
도도한 육성을 치고받는 북 장단
한 거리 당도한 곳에 아니리가 있으니

기뻐 눈물 난다고 울며 박장대소라
그득히 들어온 정 뜨겁게도 출렁여
풍상에 에굽은 낯빛 하늘다이 펴리라

*

When it comes to love, my love is *jajinmori*,❹ my breath
is short,
while my fidgeting love goes beyond *jinyangjo*.❺
Take care to add *chuimsae*❻ here and there.

Striking, twisting, with its own rythm, it dashes away.
A drum beat that beats up arrogant voices
until it reaches a place with *aniri*.❼

Weeping tears of joy, applause mingled with laughter,
affectionate feelings suddenly flood in, fluctuate hotly,
a face twisted with hardship will unfold a rainbow.

❹ *Jajinmori*: a calm and cheerful rhythm in *pansori*, etc.

❺ *Jinyangjo*: the slowest rhythm in *pansori*, etc.

❻ *Chuimsae*: brief exclamations by the audience and the
accompanying drummer during a performance, to encourage and
support the singer

❼ *Aniri*: while most of a *pansori* is sung, from time to time the singer
uses an ordinary speaking voice to comment on the action. Such
passages are known as *aniri*

*

심장을 찢어내는 우레인 줄 알았다
일순간 눈이 머는 번개인 줄 알았다

용심이 터져 나온다 센박으로 나온다

칠흑의 어둠 속을 내닫는 비봉폭포
질풍노도 삭인 후에 이슬이 되오고져

여한이 배어든 기음(氣音)* 그늘 또한 깊고녀

* 한국 소리의 특징으로 마지막 부분에 남은 숨을 거세게 뱉어서 내는 허스
키한 소리로 정과 한의 느낌을 강화시켜 준다.

*

I thought it was heart-breaking thunder,

for a moment, I thought it was blinding lightning.

An up-beat explodes, emerges as *senbak*.❽

Bibong Falls❾ that rush out into pitch-black darkness,

after life's storms and gales have calmed, become dew.

The shadow of *gieum*,❿ permeated with regret, is also deep.

❽ *Senbak*: a strong beat within a single word.

❾ Bibong Falls: a celebrated waterfall in the Diamond Mountains (Geumgangsan).

❿ *Gieum* Aspirate: A characteristic of Korean song, the husky sound produced by vigorously exhaling the remaining breath at the end of a song reinforcing feelings of *jeong* and *han*, affection and resentment.

못 잊어

불갑산 상여꽃길이
흘리는 피

상여꽃*

"요것이나 살려주면 요것이나 살려주면"**

다 삭은
흙 고무신 안

엄마와
아기가 피어

* 불갑산에 많이 자생하는 일명 상사화
**「한국전쟁 중 민간인 학살 생존자 증언—불갑산」 중에서

Unable to Forget

Bulgapsan's bier-flower paths
shedding blood.

Bier Flower, surprise lily.*

"If once you save this one, if only you save this one."**

Fully rotted
in rubber shoes of period

Mom
and baby bloom.

* So-called *sangsahwa*, which grows naturally in and around Bulgapsan Mountain
** From "Testimonies of survivors of the massacre of civilians during the Korean War—in Bulgapsan Mountain"

서울 예수

너의 죄를 사하노라
불쌍히 여기노라

우러른 머리 위에
흩날리는 꽃잎들

야위신 두 손을 들고

굽어보시는
나무

Seoul Jesus

I will forgive your sins.
I will have pity.

Scattering petals
over raised heads.

Raising two gaunt hands.

A tree
looks down.

이모식당에서

이모! 여기요, 하면
이모 생각이 나요
서방에게 매 맞아 말문을 닫아버리고
바늘에 핏물 들도록 수(繡)만 놓고 놓던 이모

수틀 위에 피어난 봉숭아꽃 질 때에
정신병원에 갇혀 소문도 없이 갔다는
그렇게 고왔다는 이모
국밥 하나 주세요

At Auntie's Restaurant

If I call: Auntie!* Over here!

I think of my own aunt,

beaten by her husband so that she never said a word,

Aunt who kept embroidering until her needle was stained

with blood.

When the balsam flowers blooming on her frame fell

she was shut up in a psychiatric hospital and died without

anyone knowing.

Pretty Auntie,

please give me some soup with rice.

* In Korea, not only the mother's sister, but also the woman who runs
a small restaurant is often called an "aunt," or *imo*.

야근하고 양말 사는 남자

캄캄한 바다에서
섬
하나가
걸어온다

희뿌옇게 떠 있는 마지막 노점 불빛

등대를 어깨에 메고
섬
하나가
걸어간다

A Man Who Works Overtime and Buys Socks

One

island

comes walking

across the dark sea.

The light of the last stall floating hazy.

Carrying a lighthouse on its shoulders

one

island

goes walking off.

절집 차

녹음이 하늘 덮어 그윽한 그늘 아래

넘치게 뜨거운 찻물 자꾸 부어주시네

씻어낼 속진의 더께가 그리 많은가요, 스님?

Temple Tea

Under the deep shade cast by greenery covering the sky

he keeps on and on pouring out hot tea.

Is there so much of the worldly dirt to be washed away,
monk?

옷가게에서

점원인가 하고 마네킹을 바라본다

마네킹인가 하고 점원을 바라본다

누군가 날 바라본다 사람인가 하고

점원인가 하고 마네킹에게 말을 건다

마네킹인가 하고 점원을 지나친다

인생이 날 지나친다 마네킹인가 하고

In a Clothes Store

I look at a mannequin, thinking it's a clerk.

I look at a clerk, thinking it's a mannequin.

Someone looks at me, thinking I'm a person.

I talk to the mannequin, thinking it's a clerk.

I pass by a clerk, thinking it's a mannequin.

Life passes me by, thinking I'm a mannequin.

토끼풀 여린 한 잎

시멘트 모래 물 뒤엉켜 돌아갈 때

아뿔싸! 휩쓸렸네
문명의 레미콘에

찢기고
으깨어지면
돌이 될 수 있을까

One Soft Clover Leaf

When water, cement and sand are being mixed together,

Oops! It got swept away.

In the ready-mixed concrete of civilization.

Once torn

and crushed,

can it become a stone?

울고 있는 풍경

콘크리트 쇠붙이 벽돌 타일 유리에

바보야, 이 바보야 눈보라는 때리고

바보야, 이 바보야…… 하며 눈시울이 젖는 골목

콘크리트 쇠붙이 벽돌 타일 유리에

춥지……, 춥지 하며 눈송이는 덮이고

아프지, 아프지 하며 온몸이 우는 도회

Crying Landscape

On concrete, iron, brick, tile, glass,

you fools, you fools, a blizzard strikes.

Saying: You fools, you fools . . . Alleys moved to tears.

Snowflakes covering concrete, iron, brick, tile, glass,

saying: You're cold . . . you're cold,

a city crying whole-heartedly, saying: It hurts, it hurts.

투신

유월 한낮 붉디붉은
수박 속 한가운데를

일순, 내지르는 칼끝
날카로운 경적

한 남자 건장한 몸을
내던졌다
수직으로

절벽에 가 부딪는
백시*의 새였는지

눈보라 자욱한 한강
생의 한가운데

날개를 찾아 헤매던
충혈된
구두 한 켤레

* 白視. 심한 눈보라나 안개로 일시 시력을 상실하는 현상.

Jumping

One midday in June
in the very middle of a bright red watermelon.

Abruptly, beneath the stabbing tip of the knife,
a sharp horn blast

a man hurled down
his burly body
vertically.

Was it a bird, lost in a white-out,
crashing into a cliff?

The Han River in a thick blizzard
in the middle of life

a pair of shoes
bloodshot
wandering in search of wings.

몽골 후기

빼곡하게 서 있는 풍경과 풍경 사이

소음에 갇혀 있는 사람과 사람 사이

대지의 빈 페이지를 갈피갈피 끼워 넣다

Epilogue in Mongolia

Between tightly packed landscapes,

between people trapped in noise,

I insert the Earth's blank pages one by one.

콜라를 마시며

몸은 여기 버리고 칼라하리로 나는 가오
탐욕의 맛이 내쏘는 단호한 창(槍) 끝에서
세 번의 빙하기 건너 푸른 화석 속으로

진정 내 몸돌은 원시의 땅, 혹여는
우주의 일망무제를 달리는 기(氣)가 되어
시원한 정의 내리리 나는 거품 아니다

비 그친 하늘에 핀 들깻잎 사이 누벼
작은 새의 폐 속에서 호오이 소리 내리오
피폐한 껍데기들이 빈 캔으로 널린 오늘날

Drinking Cola

Leaving my body here I'm off to the Kalahari.

At the tip of the resolute spear from which a taste of greed
emanates,

crossing three ice ages, into a green fossil.

Truly, my core is a pristine land, maybe

becoming the energy that runs through cosmic vastness,

I'll give you a cool definition, I'm not froth.

Crossing perilla leaves that open to the sky once rain
ceases,

I'll make a sound inside a little bird's lungs.

Exhausted husks are scattered this very day as empty
cans.

서(西)고비의 향초

대평원 고물고물 기어가는 버스 안

차창을 여니
온통
허브 향 밀려온다

저 들에 풀꽃 하나로 살아가도 좋겠다

Fragrant Herbs in the Western Gobi

In the bus crawling cross great plains.

As I open a window
all kinds of
herbal scents come wafting in.

I wish I could live as a flowering plant in those fields.

친환경 레시피

벌레 먹은 구멍도 언뜻언뜻 보이는
텃밭에 제법 익은 남새를 금방 따서
햇살과 바람 버무려 심심하고 담박하게

Eco-friendly Recipe

Having just gathered in the garden fairly well-grown
greens
where worm-eaten holes are visible at a glance,
seasoned with sunlight and wind, making them bland and
plain.

물

우리 몸이 태어나길 칠 할이 물이면

까막까치 울음과 배추흰나비 빛깔
아주 어린 벌레들과 벌레보다 작은 몸들
요세미티 공원의 숲, 몽골 초원의 들꽃
차마고도 오르는 어린 말의 순한 눈빛
그 모든 것들의 칠 할

그들을 나투게 하신
지구의 칠 할도
물

Water

If our bodies are seventy percent water at birth

Then it's also seventy percent of

the squawking of crows and magpies, the color of cabbage white butterflies,

the bodies of very young insects and bodies smaller than insects,

the forests in Yosemite Park, the wild flowers in the Mongolian steppes,

the gentle eyes of baby horses climbing the ancient mountain tea route.

So water

must be seventy percent

of the Earth that produced all those.

ALL THE DAUGHTERS OF THE EARTH 세상의 모든 딸들 ALL THE DAUGHTERS OF THE EARTH 세상의 모든 딸들

PART
4

백합의 노래

그 어떤 칼날로도 너를 열 수가 없어

연한 소금물 속에 가만히 담가두었지

세상의 이슬방울 속에 노래를 담가두었지

Song of a Clam

Since I could not open you with any blade

I quietly soaked you in mild brine.

I soaked songs in the world's dewdrops.

눈 오는 저녁의 시

어둠에 눈이 깊던 맑은 날들을 길어

내 언제 저렇도록 맹목을 위해서만

저무는 너의 유리창에 부서질 수 있을까

무섭지도 않으냐 어리고 가벼운 것아

내 정녕 어둠 속에 깨끗한 한 줄 시로만

즐겁게 뛰어내리며 무너질 수 있을까

Poem on a Snowy Evening

Drawing up clear days when eyes were deep in the darkness,

when will I manage to collide with your window in the setting sun

only for such blindness?

Aren't you scared, you young, light thing?

Will I really be able to jump and fall down happily

in the darkness, with just one pure line of poetry?

그리움

참았던 신음처럼 사립문이 닫히고

찬
이마 위에
치자꽃이 지는 밤

저만치, 그리고 귓가에

초침 소리
빗소리

Longing

The brushwood gate closes like a muffled moan.

Night when gardenia flowers fall
on the chill
forehead.

Far away, and by my ear.

A second-hand ticking.
Rain dripping.

차마고도

눈앞에 길 있으니 걷지 않을 수 없고

그대 알아버린 맘 거두어들일 수 없어

두 발이 부르트도록 구름 영봉을 넘네

The Ancient Tea Route

There's a road in front of me, so I am bound to keep walking

and since I can't harvest my heart enamored of you,

I cross cloudy sacred peaks until my feet swell.

기다림

어제오늘내일모레
어제오늘내일모레
어제오늘내일모레
어제오늘내일모레

모눈이 터질 것 같은
미친
목마름

Waiting

yesterday today tomorrow the day after tomorrow

yesterday today tomorrow the day after tomorrow

yesterday today tomorrow the day after tomorrow

yesterday today tomorrow the day after tomorrow

Crazy

thirst

as if the grid is about to explode.

아름다움의 근원

우주 먼지 알갱이가 만들어내는 별빛
못난 돌멩이들이 만들어내는 물소리

이 밤의 아름다움의 근원은

돌멩이다,
먼지다

세상 등불이 꺼진 깜깜한 어둠이라도
난 그런 돌멩이
그런 먼지다 생각하면

사랑도 혼자 가는 길도

아프지 않다
외롭지 않다

The Source of Beauty

Starlight produced by cosmic dust,
the sound of water produced by ugly stones.

The source of this night's beauty

is stones
and dust.

If I think of myself as being those stones,
that dust
in the deepest darkness when the world's lights are turned
out,

love and the road taken alone

are not painful,
are not lonely.

물소리

그대에게서 오는 물소리에 젖는다

낮잠도 노래도 물소리에 젖는다

세상이 다시 촉촉한

첫날로 설레다

단단한 두 어깨가 물 아래 흔들린다

내게서 간 물결도 그대를 적시는가

아침도 낮도 한밤도

첫날로 설레시는가

A Sound of Water

The sound of water coming from you soaks me through.

My daytime naps and my songs are soaked with a sound of water.

The world thrills again

with the first damp day.

Your tense shoulders shake beneath the water.

Are the waves leaving me making you wet?

Do dawn, day and night

thrill you as on the first day?

먼 사랑

산으로 가신다면 강으로 가렵니다
앞으로 가신다면 뒤돌아 가렵니다
지평선 끝과 끝에서 둥글게 만날 때까지

Distant Love

If you head for the mountains, I'll head for the river.

If you go forward, I'll go backward.

Until we meet in a circle at the end of the horizon.

공항에서

지구의 한끝은 어제 도착하기도 하고
지구의 또 한끝은 내일 닿기도 하는데
내일과 오늘과 어제가 정녕 다름이 없었다

컨베이어 벨트에서 멍청히 돌고 있는
어제를 사는 나와 내일을 사는 나를
모르는 짐짝처럼 두고 서둘러 빠져나오다

At the Airport

Arriving at one end of the earth yesterday,

reaching another end of the earth tomorrow,

there was really no difference between tomorrow and

today and yesterday.

Leaving behind the I who live yesterday and the I who

lives tomorrow

like an unknown piece of luggage

spinning around on a conveyor belt, I quickly get away.

내 마음속 오지

세상 구석구석을 구경하고 온 이가

가지 못한 곳만이 진정 아름답다 하길래

내게도 있다 하였지

내 마음속

오지

Wilderness in My Heart

A person who has visited every corner of the world

said that only places not visited are truly beautiful.

I said I have one like that too,

the wilderness

in my heart.

물꽃

그저
여울인 것을
바위인 당신 만나

일말
주저 없이
산산이도 부서져

당신을 감싸 안으며

나를
꽃 피웁니다

Water Flowers

It's just a shallow
but I encounter you,
a rock,

shatter
without
hesitation

and as I embrace you

you make me
bloom as flowers.

사는 힘

죽을힘으로 죄어 납작해진 넝쿨 줄기

죽을힘으로 버티던 나무 서로 뒤엉켜

녹음이 용호상박처럼 하늘을 덮더니만

부서져라 죄던 줄기 말라서 죽은 곳에

굳세던 왕소나무 넘어져 썩어 있네

인생아 가혹하여라

나,

죽을힘으로 버티게

Strength to Live

Vine stems that desperately tighten, constrict,

and trees that desperately endured, entangled together,

foliage covering the sky in a titanic struggle

but where the stems, squeezing till they snap, have dried and died,

a great pine has fallen and is rotting.

How merciless life!

As for me,

I will endure desperately.

풀잎에게 배우다

비에도 땡볕에도 바람에도
지지 않고

여린
연둣빛들
일어선다
자란다

고난은
용수철인 것
풀잎에게 배우다

Learning from Blades of Grass

In the rain, in the sun, in the wind,
undefeated.

Soft,
pale green,
they emerge,
grow.

I learn from blades of grass
that adversity is
spring.

가는 길

숨차는 아내의 손도 자주 잡아주면서
늙은 부부 꽃터널로 지팡이 짚고 갑니다

피는 꽃 피게 놔두고
지는 꽃은 지게 두고

서며 구부리며 해맑게 웃기도 하며
그 곁에 젊은 부부 유모차 밀고 갑니다

꽃잎이 흐르게 두고
어깨에 머물게 두고

On the Way

The husband holding his breathless wife's hand,

an old couple walks through a flower tunnel with canes.

Let blooming flowers bloom.

Let fading flowers fade.

Standing, bending over, smiling brightly, too,

beside them, a young couple pushes a stroller.

Let petals flow

let them settle on their shoulders.

바람이 불고 있다

겨울 오는 갈대숲에 바람이 불고 있다

고꾸라지며
뒹굴며
몸서리치는 저것은

서 있는 갈대가 아닌
그를 흔드는 바람이다

빈 벌판을 삼천 배 눕혔다 일으켰다

빛인지
그림자인지
흰 등을 내주고 있는

저것은 갈대가 아닌
아득한 시간이다

The Wind is Blowing

The wind is blowing in the reed beds where winter is
coming.

All turned upside down,
lying flat,
shuddering.

Not one reed standing,
the wind shakes them all.

The empty fields were flattened and raised three thousand
times.

Maybe light,
maybe shadow,
what gives broken backs

is not reeds
but long-lasting time.

구월

앞서가는 뒷모습
돌아 뵈는 먼 모습

보이는 것 모두
다
너인 듯싶다

아무리 숨으려 해도
숨을 데가 없이
맑다

September

Moving ahead, seen from behind,
a distant figure looking back.

Everything visible
all
seems to be you.

No matter how hard I try to hide,
you are so clear
that I have nowhere to hide.

The Ancient Novelty Called *Sijo*

Ryu Mi-ya, poet

Prefatory questions

What is poetry? Given that there are still people searching for the answer, it must be a valid question anyway. Even if they cannot be seen or heard, things that embrace the light always ask themselves questions about their existence. Let's go one step further. So, what is modern poetry? Is it a genre of literature characterized by connotations and rhymes, read or written by the people of today's Earth? Recognizing the dangers of generalization to some extent makes it easier to answer difficult and large questions. It proably is. This time, let's shift the angle of the question a bit. So, what is a good poem? When responding to this, I think I might need to adjust my posture a bit, but I think there will be little controversy about the answer itself. Surely it is "poetry that moves the human heart." Removing words to compress, hinting by allusions, and moving hearts with those kinds of unkind expressions that sometimes provoke questions rather than providing answers to life! The more you think about it, the more surprising it is that Plato tried to expel the poet from the Republic, perhaps because he saw the greatness of the poet's existence rather than the danger. Poetry cannot change the world immediately, but it does move people who change the world to enact change. Could it not have been Plato's fearful foreboding of the immense power of poetry that would shake the Republic?

Now that the global village has become a reality, in this era where material and speed have taken over and competition has become a quality, I feel a more fundamental sense of crisis than in the past about the existence of poetry and poets. In this world where economic utility and value have become absolute indicators of life, is poetry still alive?

Things unique and universal

Humans have things that come ahead of them. Those are things that exist before the birth of an individual, such as the self-consciousness of a human being, language, death, the fear of annihilation, the belief in an absolute, and the intrinsic attributes of community . . . and so on. If such priorities were not given to humans, the world would be infested with chaos and emptiness. Faced with the concrete reality of the essences that were received in advance and existed before existence, individuals and communities acquire uniqueness, and that becomes something given earlier and connected to the lives of future generations.

To Koreans, one of the things thus given is the aesthetic consciousness of the Korean language, especially the language of poetry. Since ancient times, Korean poetry has placed great importance on rhythm, and just as Koreans enjoyed dancing and singing, the poems of the old literature sway with particular and unique rhythms. Korean poetry, rooted in such a long tradition, has lasted to the present day and continues to bloom brilliantly with the representative style is *sijo*.

Sijo is as natural as inhalation and exhalation to those who speak Korean as their mother tongue. It has been maintained for nearly a thousand years as an instinctive rhythm in the bloodline of Koreans and as a unique literary tradition. In a world where globalization has been achieved through the development of transportation and communication, even now that a universal sense of life is shared with all mankind, any Korean will naturally adjust their breathing to this unique rhythm. All of the poems in this collection of poems strictly adhere to the form of such *sijo*, that is, as a standard poem, while deeply embodying the modern life of the here and now, and fully unfolding the capabilities of the *sijo* as a "modern poem," that is, as a "modern *sijo*."

What is particularly noteworthy is that these poems succeed in portraying universal human life while embodying such uniqueness of genre. That is because the poet does not hesitate to exercise her open mind and imagination not only regarding her own poetry, but also about the suffering of others and life on the other side of the world. I hope that more people around the world will be able to see the poems of this collection that contain the most Korean, most universal, and fundamental elements of life. The reader will constantly be immersed in waves of sympathy and emotion, like a beach constantly drenched in waves, while following the swaying lines in a labyrinth of moderation and blank space characteristic of the *sijo*.

A song hanging in a dewdrop

The basic form of *sijo*, termed *dansijo* means that each line contains one meaning and the poem consists of a total of three lines of meaning. The lines are called *chojang*, *jungjang*, and *jongjang*, and in terms of content, each consists of *gi* (beginning), *seung* (development), *jeon* (transition), and *gyeol* (end). If there are two or more *sijo* in this basic form, it is called *yeonsijo*, and if one line is too long, it is called *saseol sijo*. It would take up more room than is available here to fully describe the form of *sijo*, so I will just mention that much, and in what follows, I will only talk about the infinite world and depth that can be found in the short form of poetry known as *sijo*.

Since I could not open you with any blade

I quietly soaked you in mild brine.

I soaked songs in the world's dewdrops.

–Song of a Clam

The poet's consciousness of existence and the nature of life are expressed surprisingly clearly in one short poem. On the surface, "you" is a clam, but in the third line, it is revealed that it is the same as "song." It also means a song sung in the world, that is, "poetry," while overlapping again with the existence of a "poet" who sings of the world. Not even the force of "any blade" can make her open her mouth, but one day she will disappear like a daydream, and the poet who immerses herself in the "dewdrop" of the world and sings with all her being is beautifully evoked. The poet's immersive self-consciousness is revealed throughout this entire collection of poems, sometimes as personal passion, sometimes as a reflection on the past and present of communal life and an awakening towards global solidarity earth. This must arise from a deep awareness that the poet is responsible for life on earth. The following poems that show this well are works corresponding to *dansijo, yeonsijo,* and *saseol sijo,* respectively.

When water, cement and sand are being mixed together,

Oops! It got swept away.
In the ready-mixed concrete of civilization.

Once torn
and crushed,
can it become a stone?

—One Soft Clover Leaf

Leaving my body here I'm off to the Kalahari.
At the tip of the resolute spear from which a taste of greed emanates,
crossing three ice ages, into a green fossil.

Truly, my core is a pristine land, maybe

becoming the energy that runs through cosmic vastness,

I'll give you a cool definition, I'm not froth.

Crossing perilla leaves that open to the sky once rain ceases,

I'll make a sound inside a little bird's lungs.

Exhausted husks are scattered this very day as empty cans.

–Drinking Cola

If our bodies are seventy percent water at birth

Then it's also seventy percent of

the squawking of crows and magpies, the color of cabbage white butterflies,

the bodies of very young insects and bodies smaller than insects,

the forests in Yosemite Park, the wild flowers in the Mongolian steppes,

the gentle eyes of baby horses climbing the ancient mountain tea route.

So water

must be seventy percent

of the Earth that produced all those.

–Water

In particular, the third part of this collection of poems includes poems depicting Korea's unique culture or modern city life, such as "Arirang Variations," "Seoul Jesus," "In a Clothes Store," and "At Auntie's Restaurant," along with the above three poems. It is composed of works that look back on nature, life, and global life across time and space, such as "Epilogue in Mongolia," "Fragrant herbs in the Western Gobi," and "Eco-friendly Recipe." In spite of the strong restrictions imposed by the literary convention of *sijo*, poet Kim Ilyeon's poems show the climax of lively lyricism and thought through the use of fluid and clear language. This is where her writing has power. Her poetry is not the language of a palely designed laboratory, but a wondering about nature, and as you follow its clear, pulsing breath, you feel as if your soul, exhausted from the hustle and bustle of life, is being washed. Where does this sublime language come from? It is because she sets her feet on the ground of reality, but places her heart on the things of the abyss below. She quietly gazes at the things behind the landscape, not the surface. Those deep eyes evoke the rear-view of a history that has been bleeding while supporting the world.

Bulgapsan's bier-flower paths
shedding blood.

Bier Flower, surprise lily.

"If once you save this one, if only you save this one"

Fully rotted
in rubber shoes of period

Mom
and baby bloom.

—Unable to Forget

"Bier Flower" in the poem refers to the *sangsahwa* flower, which grows naturally in and near Bulgapsan Mountain in Korea. The phrase "If once you save this one, if only you save this one" is taken from the testimony of someone who survived a massacre of civilians during the Korean War. The symbols of tragedy, the "rubber shoes" and the flowers blooming, are vivid as if they were swaying in front of your eyes. The basic *dansijo* always shows a big fall between the first two lines and the last, that is, the third phrase (which is called *jongjang*), and this work also abruptly follows the presentation of the present-past scene and historical facts. An objective correlative that symbolizes the victims of the massacre of civilians suddenly appears, drawing the reader into the dark in an instant. Biers, which were used in traditional Korean funeral ceremonies, were usually decorated with "bier flowers," usually flowers made of paper. However, the *sangsahwa*, blooming at the scene of a historical tragedy (it has a name meaning that the flowers and leaves do not appear together and therefore can never meet), adds to the meaning and sadness of the poem. Why doesn't the world get better in the face of repeated historical lessons? Is the tragedy of life without learning or improvement truly unstoppable? The poet's deep gaze searches for a ray of oblique light that will make it possible, and she continues to groan.

The tasks of primal light and roots

As one of the important things "given" to humans, mentioned previously, I cannot help talking about motherhood, which is characterized by caring and devotion. It exists before the phenomenon of motherhood, just as the possibility of germination exists before the material of the seed. Beyond any simple gender distinction, it is the source of all vitality and is like the primal light that shines at the moment of birth. Its existence alone makes it possible to endure this world full of darkness.

Father used to sharpen pencils.

Mother used to iron military uniforms late into the night and a star sharpening graphite-black darkness came down into the yard.

I was told that the sound of bullets grazing past was exactly the same.

A silence terrified by a water snake entering a pond and the family was there as if lying in a tidy pencil case.

−A Star

In this poem reflecting the narrator's childhood, there are clear visual images of "graphite-black darkness" descending into the yard, of the father who "sharpens pencils," the mother "ironing military uniform," and the family "lying as if in a pencil case," together with "the sound of bullets grazing past," and "the silence terrified by a water snake entering a pond," harmonizing various senses, evoking a beautiful moment. The stillness that lies within the silence, but that it does not stop, makes this poem come to life as if it were a scene flowing from a projector in a dark space. Behind the father, a professional soldier who sharpens his daughter's pencil, and the family, who face their lives in a friendly way at the end of a tiring day, a mother who "used to iron military uniforms late into the night" stands firm. The love behind love, the longing for the mother who is the source of all love, is another earnest axis in Kim Ilyeon's poetic world.

Taking her things and leaving the house,
after closing the bank account,

terminating her mobile phone
where only my number was saved,

pocketing the senior pass I'd inherited,
feeling lonely after tears.

—A Daughter

Even if it is not based on Korean traditional filial piety, this is in line with the universal sentiment given to humans a priori. The precious things in life always come with a belated regret, and the poet likened this belated realization to "a fruitless flower" in another poem. It reminds me of the

Korean proverb, "There is only love of parents for children, no love of children for parents," but perhaps this is how great love that can make sacrifices lasts.

Hoping that you and the baby are okay,

I'm sending a stroller from Amazon to the skyscraper jungle city,

a stroller that I spent ten months choosing, a sturdy one.

—To My Daughter in New York

In this short poem, the connotation and ambiguity of poetry as "language art" are displayed in a natural and sophisticated way. Expressions such as "hoping you are okay," "stroller," and the "ten months" of pregnancy of a daughter about to give birth, together with the fact that her residence is New York, one of the largest cities in the United States and the world, attracts attention. "Amazon" is not only the name of an online shopping mall in the United States, but it is also the name of the rainforest where the largest "jungle" on the planet currently exists. Exquisitely overlapping the wild land ruled by the law of the weak, and the life of a brutal city, a scene of human alienation, it expresses the heart of a mother who cares for her daughter. No child will ever know all the motherly love of a mother who has been picking and choosing "sturdy things" for ten months. It always ends up being passed on to the next generation. The first part of this collection of poems is concerned with family bonds, memories of flesh and blood, and chronology, which shows well the worldview of poet Kim Ilyeon. It is difficult for any deep art to acquire depth without reflection on the identity of "roots." This is because only deep-rooted awareness and reflection on the origin can ultimately liberate existence from all relationships, whether it is related to flesh and blood or community. As the wind forgets the wind, as the roots forget the roots.

The ants cross it, the wind rests on it,

a flat rock with bird droppings on it,

abandoning mercy and desires, it finally achieves emancipation.

−Reclining Buddha

The poet dreams of freedom. The reason why her poems dare to sing while carrying the frame of a fixed form is because the world is, after all, a dewdrop or a pile of stones. It is because ants, wind, and people cross over it, and even a moment of time covered with bird droppings is cheerfully weathered and disappears there. The poet knows that making finite human life a journey of utmost effort and love is the way to freedom. Remembering the tasks of primal light and roots is necessary in order to be "finally emancipated."

The oldest is the newest

The Korean Wave is capturing the eyes and ears of people around the world. However, regardless of that, Korean culture has its roots in a long tradition that has ceaselessly blossomed and borne fresh fruit. The vitality and health of the group can be guaranteed when the language, which is the key to the formation of a community's culture, and literature, the essence of that language, flourishes. This is an era in which speed becomes competitiveness and culture is consumed through senses and images. In this age where everyone dreams of being an "early adopter" and applauds new products, how can there be true novelty? The real novelty comes from the roots of landscapes and objects, not their outer skins. The leaf put out by the longest-lived root is a novelty that blooms today after running for the longest time. *Sijo*, which has been the root of Korean culture for nearly a thousand years as an ever-advancing art form, and as an earth mother that nurtures present life and future liberation, is a characteristic genre that, above all, must contain vivid contemporary life. At the root of today's Hallyu is the *sijo*, which contains the identity of the Korean language and pounds in the pulse of all Koreans. The work of Kim Ilyeon, who has the creation of beautiful songs blooming as *sijo* her life's task, contains the soul and love of an artist. Now, it's the world's turn to meet the oldest and newest song, the most Korean, that resonate still as "*sijo*."

시조라는 새로움

류미야(시인)

질문의 서序

시란 무엇인가? 여전히 그 답을 찾아 헤매는 사람들이 있는 것을 보면 어쨌거나 이는 아직 유효한 질문임에 틀림없다. 보이거나 들리지 않아도 빛을 품은 것들은 늘 그렇게 스스로 존재의 질문을 던진다. 한발 더 나아가 본다. 그렇다면 현대시란 무엇인가? 지금 시대의 지구인들이 읽거나 쓰는, 함축과 운율을 특성으로 하는 문학의 한 장르인가? 일반화의 위험성을 어느 정도 인정하면 어렵고 큰 질문일수록 간단히 답할 수 있다. 그럴 것이다. 이번에는 질문의 각도를 조금 옮겨본다. 그렇다면, 좋은 시는 어떤 것인가? 이에 응답할 때는 왠지 자세를 좀 가다듬어야 할 것 같지만, 답변 자체에 대한 논란은 적을 것 같다. 아마도 그것은 '인간의 마음을 움직이는 시'일 것이다. 압축하느라 말을 뭉텅 덜어내고, 뭔가에 빗대어 에두르기도 하고, 인생에 대한 해답은커녕 때로는 질문으로 되받는 그 불친절한 표현 방식으로 마음을 움직이다니! 생각할수록 놀라운 일이다. 플라톤이 공화국에서 시인을 추방하려 했던 건 어쩌면 시인이라는 존재의 위험성보다 위대성을 간파했기 때문이리라. 시가 세상을 즉각적으로 바꿀 수는 없지만, 세상을 바꾸는 인간의 마음을 움직여 변화 쪽으로 나아갈 수 있게 한다. 공화국을 뒤흔들 강력한 시의 힘을 플라톤은 두려움 속에서 예감했던 것이 아닐까?

바야흐로 지구촌(global village)이 현실이 된 지금, 물질과 속도가 점령하고 경쟁이 속성이 된 이 시대에 왠지 시와 시인의 존재에 대해 과거보다 한층 근원적 위기감을 느끼게 된다. 경제적 효용과 가치가 절대적인 삶의 지표가 되어버린 이 세계에서 시는, 아직, 살아 있는가?

고유한 것과 보편적인 것

인간에게는 앞서 주어지는 것들이 있다. 그것은 개인의 탄생 이전에 있는 것들로, 가령 인간이 갖는 자의식, 언어, 죽음, 사별의 공포, 절대성을 향한 믿음, 공동체에 내재한 속성…… 등등이 그것이다. 만약 그런 선험성들이 인간에게 주어지지 않았다면 세상은 혼돈과 공허로 들끓을 것이다. 그렇게 미리 받은, 존재 이전에 존재하는 본질들을 구체적 현실과 맞닥뜨리며 개인과 공동체는 고유성을 획득하고, 그것은 다시금 앞서 주어지는 것들이 되어 후대의 삶과 이어진다.

한국인에게 그렇듯이 앞서 주어진 것의 하나로 한국어, 특별히 시의 언어에 대한 미의식을 들 수 있다. 예부터 한국의 시가(詩歌)는 리듬을 매우 중시해왔는데, 춤과 노래를 즐긴 겨레답게 옛 문헌 속의 시가들은 고유하고 독특한 리듬들로 출렁거린다. 이런 오랜 전통에 뿌리를 둔 한국의 시 문학이 오늘날로 이어지며 여전히 찬연한 꽃들을 피워내고 있는데, 그 대표적인 양식이 바로 시조(Sijo)이다.

'시조'는 한국어를 모어로 하는 이들에게는 들숨과 날숨처럼 자연스러운 것이다. 그것은 한국인의 핏줄기 속에서 본능적인 리듬으로, 또 고유한 문학 전통으로 천 년 가까이 지속되어 왔다. 교통과 통신의 발달로 세계화가 이루어진 지금, 보편의 생활 감각이 인류에게 공유된 마당에도 한국인이라면 누구나 자연스럽게 이 독특한 리듬에 맞춰 호흡을 가다듬게 된다. 이 시집의 시들은 모두 바로 그런 시조의 형식, 즉 정형시로서의 율격을 엄정히 지키면서도 지금—여기라는 현대의 삶을 깊이 있게 담아내며 '현대시'로서의 시조, 즉 '현대시조'로서의 역량을 마음껏 펼쳐 보여준다.

특기할 만한 점은 그런 장르적 고유성을 구현하면서도 이 시집의 시편들이 보편적인 인간의 삶을 그려내는 데 성공하고 있다는 점이다. 그것은 시인이 자신의 시정(詩情)은 물론, 타인의 고통과 세계의 이면에 대해 열린 마음과 상상력을 발휘하는 데 주저하지 않는 까닭이다. 가장 한국적이면서도 가장 보편적, 근원적인 삶을 담은 이 시집의 시들을 세계의 더 많은 사람들이 만나볼 수 있기를 바란다. 시조 특유의 절제와 여백의 미로 출렁거리는 행간을 따라가는 동안 독자들은 끊임없이 파도에 젖는 해변처럼 어느새 공감과 감동의 물결에 내내 마음을 적시게 될 것이다.

이슬방울 속에 드리운 노래

각 행이 각 하나의 의미를 담고 총 3행의 의미 시행으로 이루어지는 것을 시조의 기본형, 즉 '단시조'라 한다. 그 각각의 행을 초장, 중장, 종장이라 하며 내용상 기(시작)—승(전개)—전(전환), 결(끝)으로 구성된다. 이 기본형의 시조가 2개 이상 이어지면 '연시조', 어느 행이 많이 길어진 것을 '사설시조'라고 한다. 시조의 형식에 대해 설명하자면 지면을 다 써도 부족하니 이 정도로만 소개하고 이 글에서는 시조라는 길지 않은 시형식으로 보여줄 수 있는 무궁무진한 세계와 깊이에 대해서만 이야기하려 한다.

그 어떤 칼날로도 너를 열 수가 없어

연한 소금물 속에 가만히 담가두었지

세상의 이슬방울 속에 노래를 담가두었지

—「백합의 노래」 전문

  시인의 존재의식과 생의 속성이 짧은 한 편의 시 속에 놀랍도록 선명히 그려져 있다. '너'는 표면적으로는 백합이지만 제3행에 이르면 '노래'와 동일한 대상임이 드러난다. 그것은 또한 세상 속에서 부르는 노래 즉 '시'를 의미하는 한편, 세상이라는 대상을 노래하는 '시인'의 존재와도 다시 겹쳐진다. "그 어떤 칼날"의 완력으로도 그의 입을 열게 할 수 없지만, 언젠가는 백일몽처럼 사라지고 말 세상이라는 "이슬방울" 속에 "가만히" 몸을 담그고 온 존재를 다해 노래하는 시인의 모습이 아리도록 아름답게 그려져 있다. 시인의 이런 몰입된 자의식은 시집 곳곳에서 드러나는데, 그것은 때로 개인적 정념으로 드러나기도 하지만 때로는 공동체적 삶의 과거와 현재에 대한 성찰과 지구라는 연대적 공간을 향한 각성으로 드러나기도 한다. 그것은 시인이라는 존재가 지상의 삶에 책무를 진 자라고 하는 깊은 자각에서 비롯되었을 것이다. 그것을 잘 보여주는 다음의 시들은 형식상 각각 단시조, 연시조, 사설시조에 해당하는 작품들이다.

시멘트 모래 물 뒤엉켜 돌아갈 때

아뿔싸! 휩쓸렸네

문명의 레미콘에

찢기고
으깨어지면
돌이 될 수 있을까

　　　　　　　　　　　　　　　　　—「토끼풀 여린 한 잎」 전문

몸은 여기 버리고 칼라하리로 나는 가오
탐욕의 맛이 내쏘는 단호한 창(槍) 끝에서
세 번의 빙하기 건너 푸른 화석 속으로

진정 내 몸돌은 원시의 땅, 혹여는
우주의 일망무제를 달리는 기(氣)가 되어
시원한 정의 내리리 나는 거품 아니다

비 그친 하늘에 핀 들깻잎 사이 누벼
작은 새의 폐 속에서 호오이 소리 내리오
피폐한 껍데기들이 빈 캔으로 널린 오늘

　　　　　　　　　　　　　　　　　—「콜라를 마시며」 전문

우리 몸이 태어나길 칠 할이 물이면

까막까치 울음과 배추흰나비 빛깔
아주 어린 벌레들과 벌레보다 작은 몸들
요세미티 공원의 숲, 몽골 초원의 들꽃
차마고도 오르는 어린 말의 순한 눈빛
그 모든 것들의 칠 할

그들을 나투게 하신
지구의 칠 할도
물

—「물」 전문

　특별히 시집의 제3부는 「아리랑 변주」, 「서울 예수」, 「옷가게에서」, 「이모
식당에서」 등 한국의 고유문화나 현대적 도시의 삶을 그린 시편들과 함
께, 위의 세 작품을 포함한 「몽골 후기」, 「서(西)고비의 향초」, 「친환경 레시
피」 등 시공간을 가로지르며 자연과 생명, 지구적인 삶을 돌아보는 작품
들로 구성되어 있다. 시조라는 문학적 관습의 강력한 제약 속에서도 김일
연 시인의 시는 유려하고도 명징한 언어 사용을 통해 활달한 서정과 사
유의 극점을 보여준다. 바로 이 지점이 그의 문학이 힘을 갖는 자리다. 그
의 시는 창백하게 설계된 실험실의 언어가 아니라 자연에 근사한 것이어
서, 그 맑게 일렁이는 숨을 따라가다 보면 삶의 번다함에 지친 영혼이 씻
기는 듯 느껴진다. 이 웅숭깊은 언어는 어디에서 오는 것일까? 그것은 그
가 현실이라는 대지에 발을 붙이되 그 아래 심연의 일들에 심장을 대고

있기 때문이다. 그는 풍경의 겉면이 아닌 이면의 일들을 고요히 바라본
다. 그런 깊은 눈은 세계를 떠받치며 피 흘려온 역사의 뒷모습까지 애써
기억하며 호명해준다.

불갑산 상여꽃길이
흘리는 피

상여꽃

"요것이나 살려주면 요것이나 살려주면"

다 삭은
흙고무신 안

엄마와
아기가 피어

—「못 잊어」 전문

작품 속 '상여꽃'은 한국의 불갑산 및 인근에 많이 자생하는 일명 상사
화를 가리킨다. "요것이나 살려주면 요것이나 살려주면" 하는 구절은 한
국전쟁 중 민간인 학살에서 살아남은 생존자의 증언에서 가져왔다. 비극
의 표상인 "다 삭은 흙고무신"과 그 안에 피어난 풀꽃이 눈앞에서 흔들리
는 듯 선연하다. 기본형 단시조는 마지막, 즉 세 번째 의미 시행(앞에서 그
것을 '종장'이라 하였다)에서 언제나 앞의 두 의미 시행들과는 큰 낙차를 보

이는데, 이 작품 역시 현재—과거의 풍경과 사실(史實) 제시에 이어 급작스럽게 민간인 학살 피해자를 상징하는 객관적 상관물이 불쑥 등장하며 독자들을 순식간에 먹먹함 속으로 끌고 들어간다. 한국의 옛 상례에서 쓰인 상여에는 대개 지화(紙花)인 '상여꽃'으로 장식을 했다. 그런데 역사적 비극의 현장에 핀 상사화(하필 그 이름이 그 꽃과 잎이 함께 피지 못해 서로 그리워한다는 뜻을 지녔다.)는 시의 의미와 비감을 한층 더하고 있다. 그렇게 되풀이되는 역사적 교훈 속에서도 세계는 왜 더 나아지지 않는가? 학습도, 개선도 되지 않는 삶의 비극성은 진정 멈출 수 없는 것인가? 시인의 깊은 눈은 그것을 가능케 할 한줄기 비스듬한 빛을 찾아 계속해서 더듬으며 나아간다.

최초의 빛과 뿌리의 일들

글머리에서 언급한, 인간에게 '앞서 주어진' 중요한 것의 하나로 돌봄과 헌신을 특성으로 하는 모성(母性)을 얘기하지 않을 수 없다. 그것은 어머니라는 현상 이전에 있는 것이며, 가령 씨앗이라는 물질 이전에 존재하는 발아의 가능성 같은 것이다. 단순한 성의 구분을 넘어 그것은 모든 생명성의 원천이며 탄생의 순간에 내리쪼인 최초의 빛 같은 것이다. 그것은 존재 자체만으로도 어둠으로 가득한 이 세계를 견딜 수 있게 해준다.

연필을 깎아주시던 아버지가 계셨다

밤늦도록 군복을 다리던 어머니가 계시고

마당엔 흑연빛 어둠을 벼리는 별이 내렸다

총알 스치는 소리가 꼭 저렇다 하셨다

물뱀이 연못에 들어 소스라치는 고요

단정한 필통 속처럼 누운 가족이 있었다

—「별」 전문

　화자의 유년시절이 투영된 한 편의 시 속에 "흑연빛 어둠"이 내린 마당
과 "연필을 깎아주시"는 아버지, "군복을 다리"는 어머니, "필통 속처럼 누
운" 가족들의 선명한 시각적 이미지와, "총알 스치는 소리", "물뱀이 연못
에 들어 소스라치는 고요" 같은 다양한 감각들이 어우러지며 아름다웠던
한 시절이 인화되고 있다. 정적 속이지만 정지되지 않은 고요가 이 시를
마치 암전 속 영사기에서 흘러나오는 풍경처럼 실감 나게 한다. 딸의 연필
을 깎아주는 직업군인 아버지와, 지친 하루의 끝에서 다정히 삶을 맞대
는 가족들 뒤로는 "밤늦도록 군복을 다리"는 어머니가 꿋꿋이 버티고 있
다. 사랑의 배후가 되는 사랑, 모든 사랑의 근원인 어머니에 대한 그리움
은 김일연의 시세계의 또 하나의 간절한 한 축이 되고 있다.

짐 빼고 집 내놓고
용돈 통장 해지하고

내 번호만 찍혀 있는
휴대전화 정지하고

남기신 경로우대증 품고

울고 나니 적막하다

—「딸」 전문

굳이 한국의 전통적인 효사상에 입각하지 않더라도 이것은 인간에게
선험적으로 주어진 보편의 정서와 궤를 같이하는 것이다. 인생의 소중한
것은 항상 늦은 후회로 오기 마련인데, 시인은 이런 뒤늦은 깨달음을 또
다른 시편에서 "헛꽃"에 비유하기도 했다. 한국 속담 중 "내리사랑만 있고
치사랑은 없다"는 말을 떠올리게도 하지만, 어쩌면 이것이 희생 가능한
위대한 사랑이 영속되는 방법일 것이다.

너와 아가 모두 무탈하길 소원하며

아마존의 유모차를 마천루의 정글로

열 달을 고르고 골라 실한 것으로 보낸다

—「뉴욕에 있는 딸에게」 전문

짧은 시편 속에서 '언어예술'로서의 시어의 함축성, 중의성이 자연스럽
고도 세련된 방식으로 발휘되고 있다. 현재 뉴욕에 사는 딸이 출산을 앞
두고 있음을 "무탈하길 소원"한다든가 "유모차"와 "열 달" 등의 표현에서
알 수 있는데, 그 거주지가 하필 미국 최대이자 세계적 도시의 하나인 뉴
욕이라는 점이 눈길을 끈다. "아마존"은 미국의 온라인 쇼핑몰 이름이기
도 하지만, 현재 지구상에서 가장 큰 "정글"이 존재하는 열대우림의 이름

이기도 하다. 약육강식의 법칙이 지배하는 야생의 땅과 인간 소외의 현장인 살벌한 도시의 삶을 절묘하게 겹치며 딸을 걱정하는 어머니의 마음을 표현해내고 있다. "실한 것"으로 열 달 동안이나 고르고 또 고르는 지극한 모정을 어떤 자녀도 다 알지는 못할 것이다. 그것은 언제나 후대에 이어지는 방식으로 완성될 뿐이다. 한편, 이 시집의 제1부가 가족의 정과 혈육에 대한 기억, 연대기의 이야기로 이루어진 것은 김일연 시인의 세계관을 잘 보여주는 지점이기도 하다. 어떤 깊은 예술도 '뿌리'의 정체성에 대한 성찰 없이는 깊이를 획득하기 힘들다. 그것이 혈육과 관계된 것이든 공동체의 그것이든, 근원에 대한 뿌리 깊은 자각과 성찰만이 궁극적으로는 모든 관계로부터 존재를 해방시킬 수 있기 때문이다. 바람이 바람을 잊는 것처럼, 뿌리가 뿌리를 잊는 것처럼.

개미도 건너가고 바람도 쉬어 가는

새똥이 묻어 있는 펑퍼짐한 돌덩이

자비도 관능도 버리고 드디어 해방되었소

— 「와불」 전문

시인은 자유를 꿈꾼다. 그의 시가 굳이 정형률의 틀을 짊어지고 노래하는 것도 세상이란 결국 이슬방울이거나 펑퍼짐한 돌덩이이기 때문이다. 그 위를 개미도 바람도 사람도 건너가고, 새똥 묻은 시간의 한때도 그 위에서 명랑하게 풍화돼 사라져가고 있기 때문이다. 유한한 인간의 삶을 지극한 애씀과 사랑의 여정으로 만드는 것이야말로 자유의 길에 이르는 것임을 시인은 안다. 최초의 빛과 뿌리의 일을 기억하는 것은 "드디어 해방"되기 위해서이다.

가장 오래된 것이 가장 새롭다

어느덧 한류가 세계인의 눈과 귀를 사로잡고 있다. 그러나 그와는 무관하게 한국 문화는 오랜 전통에 그 뿌리를 두고 쉼 없이 꽃피고 새로운 열매를 맺어왔다. 공동체의 문화 형성에 핵심이 되는 언어, 또 그 언어의 정수인 문학이 번영할 때 그 집단의 생명력과 건강성은 보장받을 수 있다. 속도가 경쟁력이 되고 문화도 감각과 이미지로 소비되고 마는 시대이다. 모두가 얼리어답터를 꿈꾸고 신제품에 환호하는 이 시대에, 진정한 새로움은 어떻게 구가할 수 있는 것일까? 진정한 새로움은 풍경과 사물의 외피가 아닌 그것의 뿌리에서 온다. 가장 오래 살아온 뿌리가 내미는 잎이야말로 가장 긴 시간을 달려 오늘에 꽃핀 새로움이다. 천 년 가까운 시간을 스스로 앞서 주어진 예술의 형식으로, 또 현재의 삶과 미래의 해방을 기르는 대지적 모성으로 한국 문화의 뿌리가 되어온 시조는, 무엇보다 생생한 당대의 삶을 담아야 한다는 장르적 특성을 지니고 있다. 오늘의 한류의 뿌리에는 한국어의 정체성을 그 안에 담고 한국인의 맥박 속에서 함께 두근거려온 시조가 있다. 바로 그 시조를 일생의 과업으로 삼고 아름다운 노래의 꽃을 피워온 김일연의 시조에는 예술가의 혼과 사랑이 깃들어 있다. 이제 세계인들이 그 가장 오래되고 가장 새로운 노래, 가장 한국적이면서도 모두의 마음을 울려줄 '시조'와 만날 차례다.

About the Translators 번역자 소개

Brother Anthony of Taizé (An Sonjae) was born in 1942 in the UK. He studied at Oxford University and in 1969 he joined the Taizé Community in France. He came to Korea in 1980. He is an emeritus professor at Sogang University and a chair-professor at Dankook University. Since 1990 he has published more than sixty volumes of translated works by such esteemed Korean authors as Jeong Ho-seung, Kim Seung-Hee and J. M. Lee. He was President of the Royal Asiatic Society Korea for ten years. In 2015 he was awarded an honorary MBE by Queen Elizabeth for his contributions to Anglo-Korean relations.

안선재는 1942년 영국에서 태어나 옥스퍼드 대학에서 공부한 후 1969년에 프랑스 Taizé 공동체에 입회했다. 1980년에 한국에 왔고 현재 서강대학교 명예교수, 단국대학교 석좌교수이다. 1990년부터 정호승, 김승희, 이정명 등 한국 저명 작가들의 시와 소설을 60여 권 이상 번역하였다. 10년간 왕립아시아학회 한국지부 회장으로 재직하였고 2015년에는 한영 양국 관계 발전에 기여한 공로로 엘리자베스 여왕으로부터 명예 MBE를 수여받았다.

Credits

Author	Kim Ilyeon
Translator	Brother Anthony of Taizé
Publisher	Kim Hyunggeun
Editor	Chi Taejin
Copy Editor	Tannith Kriel
Designer	Kim Jihye, Kim Yoojung